Publishing Children's Poetry For 19 Years

Bust-A-Rhyme

Giving verse a voice

Kilkeel High School

Edited by Allison Jones

First published in Great Britain in 2010 by:

Young Writers
Remus House
Coltsfoot Drive
Peterborough
PE2 9JX
Telephone: 01733 890066
Website: www.youngwriters.co.uk

All Rights Reserved
Book Design by Spencer Hart, Ali Smith & Tim Christian
© Copyright Contributors 2010
SB ISBN 978-1-84924-843-3

Foreword

Young Writers' Bust-A-Rhyme competition is a showcase for secondary school pupils to share their poetic creativity and inspiration. Selecting the poems has been challenging and immensely rewarding. The effort and imagination invested by these young writers makes their poems a pleasure to enjoy reading time and time again.

Young Writers was established in 1991 to nurture creativity in our children and young adults, to give them an interest in poetry and an outlet to express themselves. Seeing their work in print will encourage them to keep writing and become our poets of tomorrow.

Contents

Colin McKee (11) 1	Emma Paulson (13) 42
Madison Widman (11) 2	Carly Pulford (13) 43
Lauren Moates (14) 3	Naomi Patterson (13) 44
Simon Stevenson (14) 4	Robert McCullough (14) 45
Gavin Haugh (14) 5	Claire Nicholson (14) 46
Stacie Cunningham (12) 6	Nikol Campbell (14) 47
Sarah-Jane Houston (13) 7	Hayley Johnston (14) 48
Rodney Boyd (12) 8	Louise Burns (14) 49
Matthew Clark (11) 9	Joanna Burns (14) 50
Ryan Speers (11) 10	Ruairi McKee (12) 51
John Barbour (11) 11	Abigail Nicholls (13) 52
Ruby Nugent (11) 12	Rebecca McConnell (14) 53
Matthew Moates (11) 13	Sarah Tomkins (14) 54
Mark Heelham (11) 14	Matthew Henderson (12) 55
Che Campbell (12) 15	David Beck (11) 56
Alisha Nicholson (11) 16	Rhys Clements (11) 57
Jason Shields (11) 17	Rachel Graham (11) 58
Kathryn McCullough (11) 18	Philip Annett (11) 59
Richard Hamilton (15) 19	Natalie Fisher (12) 60
Wayne Houston (15) 20	Steven Annett (15) 61
Colby Anderson (15) 21	Emily Skillen (14) 62
Ashley Johnston (15) 22	Sarah-Jane Thompson (14) 63
Abbie Cousins (15) 23	Steven Hanna (11) 64
Kirsten Patterson (12) 24	Megan Gordon (11) 65
Sophie McKee (13) 25	Amy Biddulph (11) 66
James Johnston (12) 26	Jared Green (11) 67
Ryan Wilson (12) 27	Anna Hill (11) 68
Rachel Newell (12) 28	Carol Graham (11) 69
Lyndsey Watterson (12) 29	Matthew Annett (11) 70
Chloë Lindsay (12) 30	Esther Bell (13) 71
Tara Wilson (13) 31	Rebecca Davidson (13) 72
Ryan Wilson (12) 32	Robert Barber (13) 73
Rebekka Knox (13) 33	Wilma Gordon (13) 74
Kara McKee (12) 34	Emma Johnston (13) 75
Ryan McConnell (12) 35	Naomi Haugh (14) 76
Corrie Shields (12) 36	Mark Henning (14) 77
Emma Nicholson (13) 37	Louisa Hanna (14) 78
Andrew Shields (14) 38	Carla Hamilton (13) 79
Andrew Stevenson (13) 39	Abbie Glenny (15) 80
Andrew McKee (13) 40	Joanne Cousins (15) 81
Arnold McCullough (13) 41	Rebecca Pue (15) 82

Name	Page
Rebecca Connor (16)	83
Chelsea Anderson (15)	84
Amy Morris (15)	85
Stacey Edwards (15)	86
Jeffrey Hanna (16)	87
Sarah Graham (15)	88
Stuart Watterson (16)	89
Mark Newell (13)	90
Deane Richard Hanna (11)	91
William Scott Cunningham (12)	92
Daniel McKee (12)	93
Naomi Agnew (14)	94
Ian Shannon (15)	95
Hollie Parke (14)	96
Darren Corbett (11)	97
Victoria Stevenson (11)	98
Naomi McCormick (15)	99
Courtney Burden (12)	100
Sophie Annett (11)	101
Natalie Wallace (11)	102
Bethany Hudson (12)	103
Christopher Martin (11)	104
Rhiannon Dakota Johnston (11)	105
Andrew Martin (12)	106
Annastasia Moore (14)	107
Kathryn Orr (12)	108
Victoria McConnell (11)	109
Scott Cousins (14)	110
Natalya Speers (14)	111
Chloe McCullough (14)	112
Andrew Baird (14)	113
Leah McAtee (14)	114
Lauren Annett (15)	115
Steven Gracey (14)	116
Karl Patterson (14)	117
Rachel Ogle (17)	118
Andrew Johnston (17)	119
Jenna Shields (16)	120
Rebekah Morris (16)	121
Andrew Richard Wilson (11)	122
Andre Waddell (12)	123
Naomi McConnell (11)	124
David Aplin (14)	125
Jonathan Annett (14)	126
Alan Graham (13)	127
Matthew Burns (12)	128
Chloe Hanna (12)	129
Laura Annett (12)	130
Michelle Hamilton (12)	131
Dean Hammond (13)	132
Jordan Mullan (13)	133
Louise Warnock (12)	134
Lucy Aplin (12)	135
Alexandra Moore (12)	136
Anna Graham (12)	137
Christopher Wilson (13)	138
Lynn Campbell (13)	139
Amy Burden (12)	140
David John Goodwin (12)	141
Glenn Wright (13)	142
Richard Annett (13)	143
Lynne Graham (13)	144
Laura McConnell (13)	145
Janice Graham (16)	146
David Henning (17)	147
Claudia Green (16)	148
Aaron Parke (15)	149
Ashley Cracknell (18)	150
John Finlay (17)	151
James McConnell (16)	152

The Poems

Pink

Like a shepherd's delight at night
The roses in a bush
Bright faces blushing
Newborn pigs
To me it is peaceful and calm.

Colin McKee (11)

Yellow

A warming fire of heat
Like Florida in the summer.
A cow bell dinging all day long.
A fish as long as the rainbow
Like a balloon that's playful and happy.
Exciting and bright, like the sun.

Madison Widman (11)

Lies

I never thought it would end this way,
A friendship torn apart,
You lied to me, I lied to you
And sometimes it was hard.
It was like a balloon filled with air.
Any moment would explode
So when it began to bang
Our friendship went to shreds
But after falling out with you
Something more beautiful developed
And I don't care what's in your head
'Cause he's now the one I cherish.

Lauren Moates (14)

Death

I come among the people like a thief in the night,
I knock on everyone's door,
I am the consequence of hatred and war
And can change people's lives forever.

I come quickly like a mouse,
Sometimes painfully.
I arrive at random times
And leave sadness in my footsteps.

I come when people are reckless
And also to those who are sickly.
Young people usually don't expect me,
Even the innocent cannot escape.

Most people know me,
Especially those who are old;
Some people are in fear of me,
Wondering when I will come.
I am Death.

Simon Stevenson (14)

Anger

I come among friends and pull them apart,
I cause fights and much more,
None see me, but they can feel me,
They know that I am here.

Wars are fought because of me,
I am as silent as the tide,
No one can control me,
Everyone is afraid of me.

I can guarantee a bad night's sleep,
I will hurt and control people,
I will make you unhappy,
I am anger.

Gavin Haugh (14)

St Bernard

When they're small, they're cute and cuddly,
But they soon become big and strong.
Rescue and bravery are their trademarks,
Strength and loyalty their uniform true.
A good servant to their master,
Keeping him always from disaster.
Always by your side.
To dig you out of trouble,
Carrying a little tipple,
To give you a lovely warm glow.
They are the bravest out of their pack.
They're as gentle and kind as a kitten,
But strong and mighty like a wolf.

Stacie Cunningham (12)

Ballet Exam

Pink and satin laced-up shoes
Tattered, worn and dirty
Dancing to the magical music
Round and round the floor.

My tutu sticks out
As if it was a hedgehog
As I twirl faster
You can hear my feet tiptoeing
Across the dancing floor.

At the end of my magical dance
I bow and walk out quickly
Glowing as red as strawberry
Glad it is finally all over.

Sarah-Jane Houston (13)

Blue

The colour of the sky
A blast of the waves
A bloom of berries
Blue for Stamford Bridge
A refreshing breeze
It is a calm feeling.

Rodney Boyd (12)

Yellow

A BMW as bright as a sun
Sunbathing like a burnt banana
La-La from the Teletubbies, my sister likes to watch
A sunflower blowing like a beautiful butterfly
The yoke of the egg that broke when I dropped it.

Matthew Clark (11)

Yellow

A bright summer morning, like a banana exploding.
The start of the day.
A little happy sunflower waiting to burst open,
Waiting for the sun to shine and shine.
Cuttlefish playing together,
Floating in a happy daydream.

Ryan Speers (11)

Blue

The colour of my tractor
Like a summer's bright sea
Just like the sky above
Bell-shaped flowers floating in the breeze
A dolphin swimming happily
The car zooming along.

John Barbour (11)

Red

A cute little ladybird
Like an angry face
A beautiful rose
Shining, clicking boots
Bright as my devil eyes
A sparkly crystal, like me!

Ruby Nugent (11)

Red

A danger light in a factory,
Like a house on fire,
A fire engine coming towards you,
Like blood rushing from a deep cut,
A nose bleed,
Like Hell itself.

Matthew Moates (11)

Red

The sauce on a pizza
Blood coming out of somebody's nose
The paint on a door
A big roaring fire
The cherry on a cake.

Mark Heelham (11)

Black

The colour of cats, the colour of bears,
The colour of rats, the colour of mares,
After the campfire lies the ash,
The darkness into which I dash,
A jaguar chasing after me,
Running through the darkness.

Che Campbell (12)

Blue

The beautiful sky up so high,
Graceful fish swimming around,
Sea waves blowing in the wind,
The amazing morning sky,
An ice cream running down my hand,
A peaceful rainbow's stripe so colourful.

Alisha Nicholson (11)

Yellow

The sun so bright
A big bowl of custard
Flames cracking quietly
Ugly smokers' teeth
Paint on the walls so bright
The feeling of excitement.

Jason Shields (11)

Red

A rash on someone's arm.
The bright 'stop' sign.
Gushing blood from a cut finger.
A stunning sunset
Like heat from a warm tank.
Anger from a cross teacher.

Kathryn McCullough (11)

Kilkeel High School

Nervous

Nervous is a young thirteen-year-old boy.
He is as thin as a pane of glass.
His face goes as red as blood if anyone looks at him.
He gets all his clothes out of Primark
and they are as plain as white.
He sits in the corner of the cloakrooms
eating his lunch like a spider making his web.
He hides in the corner of the room
like Kilkeel does on the map.
He stands out in the crowd like a fire on a mountain.

Richard Hamilton (15)

Boredom

Boredom is as black as coal.
Boredom is a 15-year-old boy.
Boredom is strong and muscly.
Boredom wears school uniform.
Boredom sits in school daydreaming.
Boredom just can't be bothered.
Boredom hates being in school.
Boredom talks very slow and quiet.
Boredom can't wait to get out of school and go home!

Wayne Houston (15)

Jealousy

Jealousy is a powerful thing
Jealousy is a 5ft 4, 16-year-old girl
And also quite slim
Jealousy is dull and wears plain clothes
Spying far in the distance
Walking with a slump.
She stumbles across the guy she likes
But he is with another girl
She jumps to the ground with a thump
Jealousy wishes she had what the other girl had
But she knows she can't have him
And she feels really sad.
Other people laugh
And call her a mean name
She's just a bit jealous
I'm sure you'd be the same.

Colby Anderson (15)

The Monster

She sat in the corner of the club
She stared at all the other girls
She said, 'Why not me?'
Staring at all the other girls with her dark green eyes
She was tall, skinny and wore top designer clothes
She looked all around her and she was the only girl alone
She is the green-eyed monster.

Ashley Johnston (15)

Love

I don't know how you do it
But you do it every day,
You make me love you, more and more,
With every passing day.

Your eyes are like shining stars,
That make me stare at you.
Your smile is like the morning sun,
That lights up my whole world.

I don't know how you do it
But somehow you make me
Love you even more
Than I thought possible.

Abbie Cousins (15)

Dragon

A snake with legs,
Scales like a lizard's skin,
A tail as strong as a crocodile's.
Claws like a knife's edge,
Wings like a curtain opening and closing.
Its nose, a huge black hole.
Its mouth, a cave that keeps going forever,
Its teeth, stalactites and stalagmites.
Its two feet are two massive hands
Thudding like thunder when he walks.
Going through forests
Tramping down all the trees like an elephant.
Going to his mountain with a waterfall of lava to drink.
When he is angry, he sounds like hunger.
Fire crackles inside of him.

Kirsten Patterson (12)

Dolphin . . .

Elegant and graceful gymnast,
Leaps out of the crystal-blue ocean
Into the blazing sun.

Musician to our ears,
Its sweet singing sends shivers
Down my spine.

Pearly, pale eyes are stars,
Twinkling up at me,
Picture of nature's magical beauty.

Sophie McKee (13)

The Dragon

The dragon had talons like razor-sharp knives
And teeth like stalactites
Together they mean safety to her young
And death to whomever she fights.

She flies through the sky with a whoosh to her home
A volcano, 1,000 degrees
But humans approach and she fears detection
And she flies with her young overseas.

She encounters a hunter with evil intentions
With swords and spears and much more
She fills her mouth with her deadly flames
And slays him with one mighty roar.

James Johnston (12)

Kilkeel High School

A Panda Poem

A marshmallow, dipped in black and white
Rolling around non-stop,
A white mop, cleaning up the dark dirt,
A cotton ball, wrapped in silver sand and the midnight sky.

This noble creature has thick, woolly fur
And dark, inky rings around its eyes and body,
Slowly, it munches up the bamboo it finds,
Breaking it with its strong jaws.

This respectful animal isn't very quick,
Slow it may be,
But when it tucks in its head, arms and legs
It starts rolling, swifter than a lightning bolt.

Ryan Wilson (12)

The Basilisk

Under the school and in the pipes
Something is hidden
Out of sight.

Comes from a chicken egg
Hatched under a frog

If you hear the slithering
Beware
One look and that's it.

So beware of the Basilisk
For it was born to kill.

 B eautiful but deadly
 A wful but awe-inspiring
 S lyly sneaking around
 I ll-fated legend
 L ong awaiting its freedom
 I n the chamber
 S omething stirs
 K indled anger within.

Rachel Newell (12)

The Lion

What is a lion?
Its mane, a fluffy pillow of cotton wool.
Its eyes, two glistening marbles.
Its claws, a jagged piece of barbed wire.
Its teeth, razor-sharp knives.
Its tail, a golden toilet brush.
On the ground its animal's enemy.
Hear the leaves crackle and crunch,
As they bolt through the jungle maze,
Searching for prey.

Lyndsey Watterson (12)

Monkey

Gliding through the trees with a swish and a swoosh,
Ducking and diving in and out of the bush,
Chattering and laughing and playing with friends,
In the tropical jungle, the fun never ends.

Balancing carefully on the branches of the trees,
He spies some bananas, 'Now that one's for me!'
Swooping and swinging with effortless ease,
That's how to get bananas from the tops of the trees.

Chloë Lindsay (12)

Cheetah

While men are hunting for some fur,
I prowl around the bushes
Not to be heard.
I catch a glimpse of a zebra. Dash,
Suddenly I hear a clash.
A bullet goes off and then there's a crash
As an animal hits the ground,
I run off and keep out of sight
And realise, that zebra
Has said its final goodnight.
The sun has moved on
And so must I.
And as this cheetah
I stay out of sight.

Tara Wilson (13)

Peregrine Falcon

A dark grey body,
Thin gripping talons,
Soaring majestically, above the cliffside,
Scanning the surroundings
With all-seeing eyes.

Its speed is unmatchable,
The fastest bird alive,
And he catches his prey
With a swooping dive.

It is a jet fighter,
A natural dive bomber,
A predator whose speed cannot be contested,
It is a lone hunter.

It is not a scavenger like a vulture,
It doesn't wait in silence like a spider,
It never quits the hunt
And it is like a soldier hunting down his enemy.

Ryan Wilson (12)

Kilkeel High School

Elephant

What is an elephant?
His trunk is like a snake swishing through the jungle,
His ears are stage curtains opening and closing,
His eyes are footballs in his memory-strong head,
His body is grey and smooth underneath,
His feet are weights crashing to the jungle earth.
He hears everything that goes on,
When he fights it's like lightning cracks in the sky,
When he walks it's like trucks moving down the road towards you.

Rebekka Knox (13)

The Lone Stallion

The sun reflects off his jet-black coat.
No water to be seen.
He searches with his eyes like pools of tar.
He doesn't seem that keen.

The dust retreats from beneath his hooves,
As he walks along the hot ground.
He treads on something . . .
He stops dead and looks around.

He begins to tire, so he finds some shade.
Another lonely day has passed.
Watching the sun fade,
He hopes he'll find food fast.

Kara McKee (12)

Elephant

Giant but gentle.
Legs like tree trunks,
But a slow stride.
Ears flapping, fanning itself.

Snake-like trunk, spraying water.
Thick leather skin but alert.
Making interfering blowing sound.
Ground shaking with each thunderous step.

The slapping of its cardboard-like ears,
On its thick, leather skin.
Its heavy breathing noise,
Spreads through the dense jungle.

Ryan McConnell (12)

A Penguin

They say a penguin can't fly
But a penguin doesn't need to.
A penguin may look scared and shy
But it's just like me and you.

Penguins may look funny when they walk
But they're outstanding when they swim
And even though they don't talk,
They can tell you anything.

A baby penguin, so small and sweet,
Waddles about, bumping into everything.
He's busy watching his small, clumsy feet
Then his mother calls him with a squeaky sing.

Corrie Shields (12)

Bad Bear Day!

When a bear woke up,
He gave himself a check-up
To see what he looked like that day,
But when he saw his hair
He got a big scare.

His hair was a mess
But he couldn't care less
Maybe it was for the best
So, he got dressed.

That night he said,
'I must go to bed
I hope my hair will be fine in the morning.'

When he woke up
He had a stroke of luck
His hair was better than ever before,
'That was the worst bad bear day ever!'

Emma Nicholson (13)

Opposites

Hot is the magma boiling in your head,
Cold is your teeth chattering as you dive into the Arctic,
Good is the hero rushing in at the end of the chaos,
Evil is the villain trying to ruin your life,
Black is the darkness swallowing you up,
White is the blinding light at the end of the road.

Love is the enchantment blinding a human's heart,
Hate is the curse inflicted on your victim,
Dark is the ultimate weapon confounding the enemy,
Light is the first hope lifting your spirits,
Life is your chance to make it to the top,
Death is the end, your last chance.

Andrew Shields (14)

Morning And Night

Morning is the time of day the sun rises like toast from a toaster,
It is a time when night turns into day,
When the birds sing sweetly and softly,
In the morning air.

Night is the time when the moon gives the sun a rest,
You lie in your bed, the darkness seeps into your room,
Takes control,
Your eyes shut.

Andrew Stevenson (13)

Angels And Demons

Angels and demons
The good and the bad
The life and the death
The right and wrong

The white and the black
The light and the dark
The pure and the evil
The bright and the fright

The sunshine, the moonlight
The clouds and the mist
The angels will triumph
The demons deceased.

Andrew McKee (13)

Death

Left here to rot and decay,
No one can hear me.
I want to scream but I cannot draw breath.
Would it matter if I did or not?
I feel no pain, except the pain in my still, lifeless heart.
Satan's calling is upon me.
Slipping deeper and deeper into eternal slumber.
Never-ending suffering, everlasting anguish.
What have I done to deserve this?
Is this my final day?

Arnold McCullough (13)

Concert

Heart beating like a drum
Crowd cheering louder than a plane engine
Hands sweating like a tap
Feet moving to the beat of the music
Arms swinging in my face like a propeller
Music thumping in my ears
People shoving me about like a pinball
Band playing brilliantly
A night to remember.

Emma Paulson (13)

Angels And Demons

Angels standing up above
On a big, white, fluffy cloud,
With a yellow glow shining from a halo,
Floating gracefully,
With their beautiful wings,
As you look at them they smile back,
With their lovely, pure, holy faces.

Demons crouching over, grabbing their pitchforks,
Looking at you
With their wicked grin and a devilish look
In their evil, twisted eyes
As the sinful creature creeps up on you
With their depraved, ugly face and a fiery glow
Just waiting to get you.

Carly Pulford (13)

Life Vs Death

Life is when you are free to be,
Who or what you want to be.
Life is when you're happy to be,
Just the way you are to me.

Death is when you live no more.
Death is when you are sad and sore.
Death is when you cannot be,
Who or what you used to be.

Naomi Patterson (13)

Good And Evil

Evil
Leaves a horrible feeling
A dark depraved lie
The cold cruel chill
The darkness all round

Good
The true and holy feeling
The bright righteousness of truth
A pure uncorrupt world
Total happiness.

Robert McCullough (14)

Entrance And Exit

The entrance to a life is a chance for hope,
A baby enters life and tries to cope.
The first time you enter school you're the picture of fear,
You miss your mum and want her to be near.

As we grow up our mothers get emotional too,
We tell them goodbye and go to university . . . *whoo hoo!*
The exit can be any day, right now or later on,
But I know where I'm going to . . . do you?

Claire Nicholson (14)

Anger!

Anger.
Anger is black with fury.
Anger is cold.
Anger is male.
Anger is a middle-aged, bad-tempered man.
Anger is like a growling bear.
Anger is scruffy.
Anger is like a cold, dark, damp pub.
Anger makes you scream and frightened.
Anger is tough.
Anger is inside you.

Nikol Campbell (14)

Alone In The Night

The sky is a raven.
The stars are gently emerging from the darkness.
Peeping out from behind the lit-up clouds
is the moon observing the night.
It looks as though shooting stars are racing towards me
as I try to reach my destination.
As I am serenaded by the waves
the howl and bark of dogs surprise me.
The cold air stabs at my nostrils.
I feel free and invincible in the night,
like a crow lost from its mother.
Loneliness takes over me.

Hayley Johnston (14)

Morning Time!

Wakening up in bed
like a door opening to an unknown room,
I can smell the strong sweet smell of coffee
gliding through the air to my room.
The sun is blinding me through my curtains
like car headlights on a dark night.
Sweet friendly hummingbirds bring joy to my ears
as I yawn like a car door slamming shut.
My duvet makes me feel secure,
like my nanny's china in soft, white cotton wool.
One foot out of bed
and I can feel the morning coldness eat at my toes.

Louise Burns (14)

Morning

As I half opened my tired eyes
I could see the crystal sun
Peeping through the curtains
The sweet song of birds
Echoed through the cold, chilly air
I lay curled into a ball
The duvet wrapped tightly around me
My mouth as dry as the driest sand
My feet touched the smooth carpet
As I scrambled out of the warm, cosy bed
It was morning again.

Joanna Burns (14)

Hyper

Hyper is like orange soda.
Hyper is like Coke Zero and minty like Polo's taste.
Hyper is like the sharp blade of a knife and hot rocks.
Hyper is like a light speed race car.
Hyper is like fast liquid dripping sort of gas.
Hyper is like a Transformer.

Ruairi McKee (12)

Hot And Cold

Hot
The desert floor burning my feet
The scorching sun on my face
Walking . . . barely
Searching for hope
Searching for the end of the horizon
Dehydrated.

Cold
The sound of water trickling
Trapped in a small cave
Outside a blizzard creates a clean slate
I am freezing
Very little heat left
Frostbite.

Abigail Nicholls (13)

Love/Hate

You give me confidence,
When I am shy.
You make me laugh,
When I'm about to cry.
You pick me up,
When I'm going to fall.
You cheer me up,
When I am down.
You show me love,
When others show me hate,
I think I'm in love,

You show me life,
When I feel death.
You show me the way,
I feel better every day.
You're always there,
When I need a hand.
You wipe away my tears,
And all my fears.
You say you love me,
I have never said it back,
But, I think I'm in love.

Rebecca McConnell (14)

Riches To Rags

A sea of faces pass me as I sit here on the floor,
Wondering where my next meal will come from,
Maybe the bins once more.
Don't think that I don't notice that you won't look me in the eye.
Your judgements loud and clear. Not a word. Just a sigh.

I was in the light once, on the top of my game
But wealthy and arrogant, I fell to my shame.
For in a single second you could lose everything I say.
One crisis, one disaster, one decision away.

Sarah Tomkins (14)

The Dark Night

The moon and stars glistened
And lit up the sky like a light lights up a room.
The dark night took over the evening sky.
The leaves rustled as if replying to the wind.
Owls were howling like a school bell.
The cold was like being in a freezer.
Dogs barked like wolves howling.
Clouds were big balls of cotton wool.
As I watched TV sleep took over me . . .

Matthew Henderson (12)

Rainy Day

The rain hitting my roof sounded like soldiers' footsteps
marching across concrete.
The wind was like the sky was trying to blow out a fire.
My floor screamed as I walked across it.
The heat of my fire blasted itself at me
like it was trying to punch my face.
The ticking of the clock was a man clicking his fingers.

David Beck (11)

Seashore

As I walked along the shore I could see
that the water was a hand waiting to grab me.
The taste of sand in the air was like someone eating glass.
The stones grumbled as I stepped on them.
The wind breathed into my ear.
The sea was a roaring dragon with its nostrils foaming.
As the waves crashed
it was as if an old man was giving his last breath.

Rhys Clements (11)

Ballinran Blues

Like an annoying
Little sister the
Alarm clock shrieks. The
Birds chirp with joy, 'Get
Up!' Dad hits the snooze.
Like me he must force
His feet to the floor.
The explosion of
The door as he leaves
Is my signal. Time
To move. Like a mum's
Cold hands, the thought of
School
Chills
Me.

Rachel Graham (11)

- Kilkeel High School

Homework

My mum's voice chokes me as she speaks.
I feel annoyed like an angry bear as I muse
For the answers to the homework.
The clock smiles unsympathetically as it ticks.
I listen as the trees talk to the wind in a secret code.
As I look outside I see the sun shining like a jewel.
The crisps I eat for a snack on a Saturday are like heaven right now.
I feel like gunpowder that's about to explode.
The homework destroys my happiness as I sit and work.

Philip Annett (11)

Waking Up On Holiday

The sun splitting through the curtains,
Crickets chirping like a hammer endlessly striking a nail,
Sea twinkling like the night's sky,
The smell of chlorine attacking my nostrils,
People talking like birds chirping all night long,
The smell of croissant cooking in the nearby bakery
Fills me with warmth,
The excitement in me wondering what the day will bring,
The sound of the bin lorries taking the bins away
Is like a wild animal trying to escape from a cage.

Natalie Fisher (12)

Night

The moonlight shines through my window
I can see stars lighting up the dark sky like little light bulbs
I hear owls outside hooting like there's no tomorrow
Cars outside drive by with their engines humming
I lie in bed wishing there was no school in the morning
A lie-in would be great
The clock is ticking, I should be sleeping
I drift into a deep sleep dreaming of no more school.

Steven Annett (15)

The Escape

Everyone's running, running to escape,
Their screams go right through me,
And their chitter-chatter constantly going, never ever ending,
Bashing, crashing, pushed out of the way,
Not knowing which way to turn,
It's all a maze to me,
Clinging to my bag,
Desperate not to let go,
The taste of damp fills my lungs,
As I run and run and run,
The unmissable smell of the dark dreary corridors,
It's getting further and further behind me,
The gates are now in sight,
So close,
But so little time,
Footsteps crashing all around me,
I'm out,
It's over,
I've escaped!

Emily Skillen (14)

7am

Awoken from a deep sleep,
by my aggressive alarm clock.
Nature creeps in with birds singing softly,
roosters crowing.
The burnt toast filters through my door,
assaulting my senses.
Bright light blinds my eyes like the Caribbean sun.
Rubbing my tired eyes, I feel weak.
Struggling to get out of my warm bed.
'Get up!' shouts a distant voice.
Just five more minutes.

Sarah-Jane Thompson (14)

In The Morning

The telephone wire shakes like a skipping rope.
Toothpaste forms a burning fire inside my mouth.
The kettle downstairs is like a steam train breaking.
The bed holds me as I try to get up
And the duvet is over me like a net.
The birds sing loudly as I eventually get up.
The smell of soap swims up my nose
And hits me with the scent of cleanliness.
I hear the TV blasting like a rock band every morning.
Toast jumps and rings a bell when it is ready.
Milk is like a thick, pure, flowing river.
The carpet is a sheep's woolly coat.
Water runs through my fingers like a waterfall.

Steven Hanna (11)

Kilkeel High School

By The Water's Side

On the sandy beach by the water's side,
Some sharp rocks like glass I spy.
The gushing waves are sea lions roaring
Out in the canoe, it's definitely not boring.
Up pops a seal, bobbing like a buoy.
The puddles are drowning people splashing in panic.
Back we go, then we jump in the sea.
Oh the taste of the salt from the sea,
It tastes like chips with far too much salt and vinegar.
The sea is not warm but it is not too cold,
I think it is just right for me!
When I dive down deep it's a jungle underwater,
It's a lovely sight!
It's time for dinner, let's go!
I feel the sand between my toes.
It's a feather tickling my feet.
Now for the hot dogs that I must eat.
Laughing and giggling, that does not stop,
As if someone keeps repeating it.
The lovely sounds and sights on the beach,
I wish it could last forever.

Megan Gordon (11)

Winter's Night

The street lights come on like an extra pair of eyes in the sky.
Ice on the ground like a bed of broken glass.
The cold air flows from the Antarctic.
Inside is all warm and cosy as if you're hugging a hot water bottle.
The smell of the Christmas cinnamon candle invades my nostrils.
Taste the Quality Streets as they melt in my mouth.
Crackling as it goes, the fire burns on.
The Christmas songs play all night with everyone singing along.
As the Christmas tree wobbles the presents hold it down in place.

Amy Biddulph (11)

Kilkeel High School

In The House

I walked into the empty house, it was like a lonely desert.
The TV was talking to me with its bright face.
My schoolbag was bursting like a bomb ready to explode.
The cold table was like an icicle falling from the heavens above.
I was tired and my bed was whispering to me to fall asleep.
I could still taste the ice cream's creamy goodness
and my stomach was yelling at me to get more.
The farm outside smelt like rotten cheese
with evil flies greedily nibbling away.
I was bored like a sheep with nothing to do.
I lifted the TV remote, it sent signals
like a whale in the ocean talking to its friends.

Jared Green (11)

When The Bell Rings

The bell rings and I hear the sound of children shouting
like the sound of an aeroplane taking off.
And then the teacher's sighing with relief
like a kettle when it is coming up to the boil.
Then when I get up, the weight of my schoolbag
with all the homework is as heavy as a ten tonne elephant.
All the friends talking as they come out of class
as happy as the sun to be going home.
Friends split up and rush for the bus like a herd of animals.
Bus fumes coming out of the bus
smelling like smelly socks and dancing in puffs of smoke.
On the bus,
sit down and you are as happy as spring.

Anna Hill (11)

Dust A Rhyme - Kilkeel High School

I Feel Free . . .

The sweet, gentle smell fills my lungs with comfort.
I enter the arena.
Dust enters in and out of my mouth
Like a river flowing through a tunnel.
The thump of the hooves beat in time with my heart.
The excitement is filling up inside me.
The jump is getting closer and closer . . .
I turn the final corner
The jump is now staring at me with challenging eyes.
I take the jump.
My mind clears.
I feel free . . .

Carol Graham (11)

When I Wake Up

The quilt jumps off me and I get out of bed.
The floor creaks like an old man dying.
I walk along the hall towards the kitchen.
My shoulders feel like a tonne weight pushing me to the floor.
I walk into the kitchen and sit down at the table.
I hear the toast jumping out of the toaster.
I lift up the cereal box,
The cereal jumps for freedom and into my bowl.
I open my mouth to eat the cereal,
It's a huge cave full of slime that journeys to the unknown.
I turn on the TV, it opens its eyes and begins to talk.
I am ready for another day of school.

Matthew Annett (11)

The Morning Sun

The alarm clock rang like a fire bell, warning me to get out.
So I tried to open my eyes but they were too heavy.
It was like trying to open a door with no key.
The covers around me seemed so warm and comforting,
It was hard to resist but I just pushed the clinging arms away
And stumbled my way to the window
And pulled away the barrier, that was the curtains
And revealed the blinding, yet beautiful sunlight.
The sunlight flooded the room with its light and warmth.
Behind the sun shining over the dark mountains.
The mountains were like sleeping giants
That were yet to be wakened.
The light bounced off the wet fields of green.
It shimmered off the dancing grass in the wind.
The little houses almost hidden in the mountains
Were still sleeping, lazily yet peacefully.
Suddenly, from the corner of my eye
I saw the birds flying high above,
In their groups, like their own army in the sky,
Flying freely and fearlessly.

Esther Bell (13)

Struggling To Wake Up

I'm lost, I'm trapped.
Trapped in a labyrinth of material
A cage of suffocating fabric holding me alone.
Where am I? Where's the exit?
Can't stay here, must escape . . .

Shrill tweets penetrate my prison,
Serrated knives piercing my consciousness.
A banshee joins the screeching knives,
Screaming her tormented lament.
Over and over again . . .

A dim figure stirs in my mind,
Reaching out to me from the shadows
With dark, calloused hands,
Threatening to crush me.
But I can't remember why . . .

My eyes open, bright light dazzles me,
Stuns and shocks me,
Splashes onto the walls,
Like paint across a canvas
I need to get up . . .

Rebecca Davidson (13)

- Kilkeel High School

Nature

The birds swayed around me in formation
like synchronised paratroopers,
all the while screaming commands at each other.
Mountains around me were great leviathans
rising up from the earth.
The racing wind beat against my body
like a wall of air refusing to let me progress on my journey.
My muscles, the pistons of an engine,
pumped the pedals round on my bike.
Clouds split and beams of sunlight shone through,
Sunlight bathed my face with her motherly, warming touch.
After seeing this beauty I felt a great peace
sweep over me like a sea of serenity.

Robert Barber (13)

Dusk

Tiredness overcomes my eyes,
My mind is peaceful, still and calm.
Pink clouds scatter the sky,
As the sun sets behind the silhouette mountains
Leaving a rainbow of colours.
Sprayed across the sky,
Sparrows perform their final synchronised show.
Time freezes still like a clock that doesn't tick,
A dark black curtain covers the purple sky
Leaving only total darkness.
There is then silence, complete darkness.

Wilma Gordon (13)

Rise And Shine

An image emerged from my eyes as I arose.
Bright colours scattered across the cloudy sky.
The blistering wind rustled through the trees as if they were at war.
Birds chirped as if they were having a conversation with each other.
The clock ticked in my ear like it was trying to threaten me.
Excitement ran through me as if it was running a marathon.
I was ready for the big day to come.

Emma Johnston (13)

Sunrise To Sunset

The sea . . . a newborn bird, no thought, just calm.
The wind . . . so quiet, it whispers its voices to me.
Cars . . . whizz and buzz, why the rush?

In the distance, the mountains look icy and cold,
Like a man swimming the Arctic waters.

What a peaceful part of the day that awakens . . .
Wait 'til I get to school.

Naomi Haugh (14)

The Starting

The day's starting, the sound of birds chirping.
The sound of cars driving off
towards what feels like an endless day.
The warmth of the sheets dragging you back
from escaping its tight grasp.
Suddenly the dreaded feeling of going to school.
The smell of toast freshly made
coming through to attack your tastebuds.
The tiredness starts to creep away
like a thief for another day.

Mark Henning (14)

Broken Sleep

Consciousness shakes me as my mind begins to animate again.
In the distance I can hear my alarm ringing like background music.
It feels like night.
Then I hear the dog barking like an unremitting siren.
The light from outside is an explosion entering my room.

Louisa Hanna (14)

Emerge

The morning light shines through the blinds
forcing them to open.

I hear the chirping birds outside
like musical instruments in the sky.

My alarm rings,
it is my morning siren reminding me not to sleep in.
The echo of the banging doors below
crawl up the wall beside me.

Tiredness from the night before drains from me like an oil leak.
After all the wake-up signs, my eyes begin to flutter open
to face the day that lies ahead.

Carla Hamilton (13)

My Miracle

Frizzy, curly or just plain straight,
They effect they have will be great.
Straight, perfect, silky hair,
Instead of looking like a grizzly bear!

60, 100, 210,
feel the heat rising.

For a party or a date,
Your hair can't be straight,
Be the envy of all your friends,
Use GHDs
Start a new trend.
Purple, pink, what do you think?

They allow you to be who you want to be!

Remember,
Straight ain't great!

Abbie Glenny (15)

Kilkeel High School

BOGOF - It's A Rip Off

Wonderful waterfalls of
Icy, clear rain,
tumble and twist.
Mountain fresh,
bursting with life
free for the taking.

But soon . . .
New flavours,
Improved bottle,
Half price,
'Get yours while stocks last!'

Out of the tap and into the bottle
how come we pay for it twice?

Joanne Cousins (15)

Water, Water, Water

In need of light refreshment?
In need of a healthy choice?
In need of a pocket-friendly option?
Too cold to hold,
Step up and enter the world of beauty in a bottle.

It sits on the shelf and stands out a mile,
Overpowering lesser liquids
With its eye-catching colours
And sexy slogan,
Water! Water! Water!
Gurgling towards your teeth; the icy coldness,
Sends shivers down your spine.

The future's light,
The future's liquid!

Rebecca Pue (15)

War

War is a waste of time!
People suffer and lose their lives
And what for? Nothing!
Out in the battlefield it goes on and on,
Got no time to stop and talk.
Dead bodies everywhere.
People shouting, screaming
Guns going off.
Quickly having to put on your gas mask
Before it reaches you.
Have to watch you friends die in front of you
If they were too late.
War is a waste of time,
Is it worth all the pain?

Rebecca Connor (16)

Another Day

The night is cold, the stars are bright, all is silent
The only noise is the low grumble of the men's stomachs, in the distance.
Mud oozes around our boots, as we return from the front line
Young men, giving their lives and for what?
A better world? Pride? Honour?
War is nothing to be proud of, like lambs to the slaughter we are.

The sun is rising, blood and bodies clearly visible now.
Grass is no longer green, but an earth-shattering shade of red.
Men, no not men, boys, drag themselves up from their slumber
Reporting to the all too familiar posts, preparing for another day.
A day sure to be filled with loss, agony and sorrow.

Barely into adulthood, I can see the life drawn from their faces.
How they yearn to be home, if it still exists, with family and friends.
What was left for us when the war was over?
A thought none of us please to think about.
A gut-wrenching image comes to mind, are they all dead?

Guns echoing, forever ongoing, it's nearly time for me to join them.
Another day, another battle, another uncertain fate.
Is today possibly the last day I spend in this wretched war?
Anything must be better than this, a life of torment and suffering.
A world of peace, will I ever see it again?

Chelsea Anderson (15)

- Kilkeel High School

Unknown

The nightmares, the dreams
Come in the night.
Visions of death fill the mind
Consuming, controlling.

Visions of soldiers, fighting, dying
Screaming, shouting.
Longing for a land they may never return to
For a child they may never know.

Bodies blown to pieces
Soldiers shot down
Lying numbly on the ground
Whilst their blood flows all around.

Survivors deal with it as best they can
But they will never be the same.
The nightmares, the dreams are always there
Lurking in the shadows of the mind.

The families of the deceased are in mourning
Hoping it is only a dream.
That soon they will wake up
And everything will be as it had been.

Amy Morris (15)

The Battlefield

Blood, blood everywhere,
But there's nothing more I can do.
Men continue frowning,
While the gas continues drowning.
Afghan, Iraq, what more can we put these soldiers through?

Hear the cries of the voices in the wind,
Hear the sound of explosions below your feet.
Soldiers are dying,
Whilst babies are crying.
Who is lost, a husband, a brother, a friend?

As the sun dies down over the blanket of dead soldiers,
Mussel flashes illuminate the sky.
The soldiers no longer age,
But the families grow in rage,
Then home they will go to a life of pain.

Stacey Edwards (15)

The Men In Red

The soldiers marched
trudging their boots behind.
mortars crashed like breaking waves,
as one by one they drop like flies.

Blood, gunshots!
As they flounder for shelter,
though those chosen few
do not make it on time.
Where did it go wrong?

Men, innocent men,
who were once loved and cared for
though now seem to be worthless,
don't your wives understand,
these are your men?

The blood covers the trenches
from mud to a red sod.

Can't you hear the cries of these men,
suffering in agony?
Protect them, love them, care for them.
Afghanistan, Iraq, Iran, *stop!*

Jeffrey Hanna (16)

War

All was silent across the dusty war field,
the once soothing sound felt like a nightmare,
what was going on? Why silence?
Men were waking from their well-deserved naps,
something was happening.

A quiet hissing sound was escaping from the trench,
after the painful silence there was no total chaos,
running, shouting, fighting arguing,
where to go, what to do?

The gas was a smothering, green blanket,
the choking sounds of suffocation
were almost piercing.

Sarah Graham (15)

Thirst No More

Still, shining, sparkling water,
runs smoothly from the
hills of Scotland.

Handy size! Multipack!
Great with a snack!
Flip up your cap!
Improve your fitness
And top up from the tap.

Drunk in Ireland,
Bottled in Wales,
So, thirst no more!
Enjoy it as you're
refreshed once again.

Stuart Watterson (16)

Attractagirl

For men about town,
The strongest hold ever,
Forget tidy,
Ignore stick,
Let's go for *sexy!*
Messy, mad and manly,
High 5 to style.
Beat your mates to the
Best girl in the class.
Attractagirl!
Turns the prom queen
Into putty in your hands.

(Hurry while stocks last!)

Mark Newell (13)

The Moon Is . . .

A white beam of light.
An icy sphere.
A circle of cheese.
A ball of flour.
A star's hotel.
A mate of the sun.
The place with no living.
A friendly face and a giant rock floating in space.
A big ball of bubblegum.
A bowl of porridge.
A white, bright light.
A white, big bowling ball.
Death.
A snowball.
A person who needs a friend.
A white banana in the sky.
The moon is a lovely, white shadow.
A big, white rock, floating in space.
Another world.
An everlasting light.
A storyteller.
The moon is a mystery.
A scary symbol when it is full.

Deane Richard Hanna (11)

The Moon Is . . .

High in the sky
Covered in craters
A big ball of cheese
A big yellow ball
Above the world
Like a light in the sky
Surrounded by stars
Round
Bigger than the Earth
Out at night
In space
Like a ping pong ball
Deserted
Orbited by Earth
Uninhabited
Visible from Earth
The moon is a planet.

William Scott Cunningham (12)

A Thunderstorm Is . . .

Crashing cars
A flash of light
A wild duck chase
A sky's nightmare
A dark night
A blacksmith making gates
Deadly to electricity
Fierce and spiteful
A car racing the streets
A cry from the clouds
A bottle of shock
A cover of torture
A trainee electrician
A clash of drums
A realm of darkness
Full of force
A form of evil
A curse from Hell
A farmer's nightmare
Crops' death
A tree's end.

Daniel McKee (12)

The Beach

Warm wind blows all around me,
baked sand burns beneath my feet,
the sun shines down upon me,
as I walk along the beach.

With sea spray splashing around them,
children play joyfully, in the sand,
whilst others run around them,
spades grasped tightly in their hands.

The sun dips down into the waves,
it's the closing of the day,
as the beach turns ghastly grey,
the crowds all drift away.

Naomi Agnew (14)

Why

Dead bodies lie,
Still people cry.
Graveyards are full,
But why? But why?

Black suits and ties,
Come to our eyes,
Large coffins lifted by depressed crowds,
But why? But why?

Soon there's tearful eyes,
As one man dies,
Sad people follow a large, brown coffin,
But why? But why?

Man's fatal hands,
Harm opponent's bands,
Those deadly guns take precious lives,
But why? But why?

At the end of the day,
When the battles are all won,
When fierce soldiers have nowhere to roam,
Sin has left its bloody mark,
That's why. That's why.

Ian Shannon (15)

Morning

The annoying noise of the alarm,
Buzzing in my ear,
The curtains swing open
To let the new day in.

The rising of the sun,
Shining brightly in my room,
The hustle of the traffic outside,
Is telling me I need to move.

The birds outside the window,
Whistling a random tune.
The noise of the rooster,
Doing its ongoing tune.

The comfy feel of the duvet,
Just won't let me go.
The smell of a cooked breakfast,
Is telling me I should go.

Hollie Parke (14)

The Sun Is . . .

A big ball of cheese
A massive beach ball
A bloodshot eye
A sinking hot air balloon
An exploding orange
An end of a red-hot poker
An end of a burning cigarette
A giant fire ball
A blazing hot sphere
The world's cheapest source of light
A bright glow of a candle
A giant baseball
A giant tennis ball
An orange hockey ball
A massive, yellow football
A gigantic light bulb
A giant, yellow apple
A ball of lightning
A big, spiky ball
A brighter moon
A giant, yellow face
A blob of yellow Blu-Tack
A big ball of gum.

Darren Corbett (11)

The Moon Is . . .

A snowball that is waiting to be thrown at you,
Scary and unknown,
A circle of snow,
A place beyond the sky,
A bouncy ball,
A place where aliens live,
Death,
Loneliness,
A ball that stays up in the sky,
A grey circle of cloud,
A cloud that is grey,
Another world waiting to be discovered,
A grey blanket in the distance,
A soft, silky pillow,
A grizzly bear that wants to lift you,
Silence,
A big person that wants to have a friend,
A smiling face with grey hair,
A place where light can't show.

Victoria Stevenson (11)

Kilkeel High School

War

War is everything we see all the time.
As the clock hands go round,
Bang!
Someone or something is blown up.
Before time can move again
People fighting for what they believe in.
Children crying in doorways,
Wondering when their daddy is coming home.

Naomi McCormick (15)

The Sun Is . . .

A light ball
A firework
A blanket
A diamond
Popcorn
A bright star
A crispy bun
An orange carpet
A highlighter
A bumblebee
A school bus
A buzzer
A mermaid's tail
A bouncy ball
A bowl of porridge
A hair band
Vanilla and chocolate ice cream
A crown of gold
Yellow chewing gum
Orange chewing gum
A bucket
A magical kingdom
Cheese
A football shirt.

Courtney Burden (12)

The Sun Is . . .

A giant light bulb,
A blinding shock,
A bouncy ball,
An enormous firebomb,
A bright star,
The inside of popcorn,
A magical kingdom,
A crispy cake,
The blasting of a firework,
A soft, soft blanket,
The brightness of the horizon,
A daffodil,
A bowl of vanilla ice cream,
A yellow highlighter,
A school bus,
A yellow bumblebee,
The inside of the diamond.

Sophie Annett (11)

The Moon Is . . .

A softly glowing pearl,
A light in the middle of darkness,
A humungous ball of cheese,
A ball of shining lights,
A guiding light for the world,
A glowing ball of mist,
A cotton ball in the midnight sky,
A ball of explosive gases,
God's eye looking over us,
The sun's twin,
A werewolf's sign,
A ball of sparkling wool,
A ball of snow.

Natalie Wallace (11)

The Ballet Dancer Is . . .

A cloud flying round the stage,
A TV show you just can't stop watching,
The start of a show-stopping performance,
A child's dream coming true,
A bunny that just can't stop
The point of a dance teacher's life,
A sparkle that can't go dull,
A heart being filled with joy,
A job well done,
The beginning of a new life,
Putting a smile on people's faces,
A bright light you can't miss,
A happy ever after,
The end of a good day,
Why you get up in the morning
And a dream of mine.

Bethany Hudson (12)

The Moon Is . . .

Dark's embrace,
The darkness surrounding the sun,
A torch in the sky,
Light in pure darkness,
A friend in loneliness,
Life anew,
Death's kiss,
Time for mischief,
Freedom,
Swiss cheese,
A wolf's howl,
A thief's playground,
The sun's son,
A diamond in the sky,
Angel's meeting spot,
A sea of blue,
Foggy glass,
A pearl in the sky,
The brightest star,
A reflection on life,
The night's sun,
A light in darkness,
The king of the night,
Time to sleep.

Christopher Martin (11)

- Kilkeel High School

The Moon Is . . .

A ball of crystal,
A ball of puff,
A shining light bulb,
A flash of light,
A dog's bark,
A surrounding earthquake,
A key turning,
A torch in the sky,
An owl hooting,
A bright shape,
A distant object,
A shimmering reflection.

Rhiannon Dakota Johnston (11)

The Sun Is . . .

A pot of gold,
A fiery furnace,
A ray of light from Heaven,
A bright circle,
A yellow ball of heat,
Twelve hours of fun,
A stunning show,
A massive, yellow football,
A fiery planet,
A warm spot on the Earth,
A firework,
A school bus,
A king's crown,
A gold ring,
A shiny set of teeth,
The World Cup,
A special medal,
The world's light bulb,
And
A large projector.

Andrew Martin (12)

The End

The air was thick and black, with a faint hint of grey.
The stars were hidden beneath the blanket of mist
covering any source of light.
The only ray of light to show was from the ball of fire called moon.
The moon stood superior over the dark sky
and caused a beam of light to shine over the graveyard.

The graveyard lay silent and the wind did not blow,
The aura of death lurked around this morbid scene.
All life had been sucked from this enclosure,
It had left nothing but a few violated tombstones.

Suddenly, from beneath the grave, rose a dead, deformed figure,
It stood tall and large but shook as if possessed.
The figure emerged from its position of rest and jutted towards me.
It came slow and unsteady, closer and closer to me.
I could do no more.

Annastasia Moore (14)

The Sun Is . . .

A light bulb in the sky,
a beautiful bright tulip,
mustard,
strong, with warmth,
fun,
flames,
a fire in space,
something yellow,
flames in outer space,
a blanket of yellow,
a sunflower,
a treat,
bright,
beating on the sea,
a yellow, bouncy ball,
a bright, magical kingdom,
an exploding yellow,
a blazing hot sphere,
mighty,
full of pride,
blazing hot,
furious,
adventure.

Kathryn Orr (12)

Kilkeel High School

The Sun Is . . .

A tennis ball,
happiness and friendship,
a shining star,
a summer's morning,
a hot water bottle,
no sadness,
a bright light bulb,
a yellow wall,
full of life,
spirit-lifting,
a juicy orange,
a bright torch.

Victoria McConnell (11)

Silent Skiffs

Full moon rising over the horizon
As dozens of silent shadows skim
The surface of the deep, plentiful
Sea.

The sounder does its magic
And shoals of the silver darlings
Are located for the kill.

The ships haul up their nets with
5 cran each. When the sun is rising
the ships head to port, with a treasure trove
of the silver darlings.

Scott Cousins (14)

Kilkeel High School

Frightful

Walked in through the door
Expecting to see his bubbly, cheerful face.
I didn't know what lurked my way
But it was going to be an unforgettable experience.
Gruesome blood coated his bed
He looked ghastly, lying lifeless.
Terrified, I wanted to escape this horrific nightmare.
I was panic-stricken,
In case he wouldn't live.
Stabbed!
Would he ever be normal again?
Out of my secure fairy tale
In this different world.

Natalya Speers (14)

The Dog

Just a typical day
Bored out of my wits,
Dad and I went on our normal bike ride
But it wouldn't turn out that way.
Nearly home and totally exhausted.
Suddenly . . .
A gigantic dog sprinted out
And I couldn't brake in time
I was ripped out of my seat as if
Someone had opened their chocolate bar.
Flung straight into the air
Landed in a heap with dog grovelling over me.
Thought I was going to die
Almost ripped my face off.
But Dad saved me.
I ended up with only this ugly, black eye.
I'll never forget this ghastly day.

Chloe McCullough (14)

\- Kilkeel High School

The Flood

Is was so still, quiet and peaceful,
All of a sudden the heavens opened.
It poured with rain,
The rivers were swollen.

There was an almighty flood, huge in size,
In a large, substantial river.
So strong and powerful,
So loud, that it scared every living thing, far and near.

Everything extremely dramatic,
Everyone so shocked, stunned and scared.
Boulders tumbling down the mountainside,
The black, ferocious looking sky never seemed to leave,
But then . . .

When morning arrived, everything was so bright and calm,
The river small and gentle,
Everything so quiet.

Andrew Baird (14)

Chased

Scorching hot day,
Sun beaming down, blinding what was clear.
Shocked at what I saw.
Chased . . .
Sprinting so fast I could feel the heat rising through my feet.
Aching pain of tiredness.
Not knowing where to go.
Terrified, shaking.
Panting for breath.
Searching for something I hope I'd never find.
Amazed I got away.

Leah McAtee (14)

Saved

I stood, gazing into the deep, mysterious water
Very anxious, I lowered myself in.
The crystal clear, blue water dazzled my eyes
The sparkling shine mocking my reflection.
Suddenly the waves became extremely rough
That calm, beautiful water now an ugly, stormy sea.
Terrified, I tried to swim with all my might.
The waves would not give in.

My heart thumped in a moment of terror
I was losing hope
I remember seeing a big, tall man
A lifeguard had reacted quickly and now I was safe from danger.

Lauren Annett (15)

Mountain Horror

Our mountain climbing experience went totally wrong.
A peaceful afternoon, walking in the Mournes
was meant to be exhilarating, not terrifying.
Mist closing in, my dad thought he had found a shortcut to the top.
But the giant cliff face looked petrifying.
Was he wrong?
Clambering towards the summit,
Shingle began to toll beneath our feet.
Each movement caused a miniature rock slide.
My fingers were freezing, numbed by the chilly mountain air,
We would never survive the fall.
There was no way down, we had to keep going up.
Talk about living on the edge!
Were we all alone or was help at hand?
This was not the adventure we had planned.

Steven Gracey (14)

Kilkeel High School

Barbed Wire

It was a sunny but a very windy day also.
I was at home, playing with my sister in the garden.
The trees were swaying in the wind,
Back and forward, back and forward, whilst we were playing.
Suddenly the game turned ugly
And I had to run for my life.
I jumped onto the wall where I thought I was safe,
Until, out of nowhere,
I heard a crack,
Then another, until suddenly it broke.
I suddenly realised that I was in deep trouble.
I fell onto a sharp, rusted, barbed wire fence.
I looked down and saw red, rosy blood
Running down my leg.
I nearly fainted.
I shouldn't have jumped; I felt so stupid afterwards.
It looked unrepairable.
I couldn't believe what had happened.

Karl Patterson (14)

Learn From Their Mistakes

The letdown of the family,
The ugly child,
But the child with ambition,
One that could have stood out from the crowd.
To her mother, she was the cause of all faults
And to her father, non-existent,
Love was all she longed for,
But abuse is what was real.
Alone.
Alone is how she felt.
Her empty heart was filled with guilt,
Her heart, twisted and torn with envy towards others,
But to herself she kept it,
Pity was a weakness indeed, being hurt was her strength,
Living only in an atmosphere of hatred,
Of abandonment,
She was confused and misunderstood,
Was her future being painted?
These are memories of her past,
Determined not to make them her future.
From their mistakes she'd learnt,
Alone,
But alone no more,
She'd decided everything must happen for a reason,
Hers being;
This won't be my future.

Rachel Ogle (17)

Death

That word; that single menacing word,
Bringing fear, terrifying cries to all;
To all it takes a grasp of.
Unbearable feelings that come with loss,
The loss of a loved one, the pain within uncontrollable.

That one moment - 'I'm sorry but . . .'
Cuts you in two, smashes your heart in two.
Now you're thinking, *What shall I do?*
To prepare for the days ahead,
The few days left with your loved one.

Tears in full flow as people flock,
To say their final farewell.
The pain is uncontrollable,
Wishing they were beside you,
To comfort you in these painful days.

That dreaded day arrives, that single,
Feared day you wished would never happen.
To see your loved one carried for his final journey.
Then comes the final farewell;
Death, that destructive character that never stops!

Their memories still with them but death,
Has ripped them apart from the good in their lives.

Andrew Johnston (17)

Music

Music reflects personality,
It can show real feelings and true emotion,
Music is more than a sound,
But a passion, a hope and special meaning.

Music can bring people together,
It can be friendship, a bond and closeness,
Music can be a getaway,
An escape, and a chance for real freedom.

Music can trigger an emotion,
An excitement, a rush and a passion.
Music can change someone's mood
Bringing back memories or a special feeling.

Jenna Shields (16)

Kilkeel High School

Friends

Do you ever just sit and wonder what life would be like,
Without those little things we take for granted?
That 'hi' in the corridor on the way to your next class,
The little 'what you up to?' text in the evenings,
And the random phone calls in the middle of the night.
These silly little everyday things, you don't even stop to think about.

Then there are the other things,
Those things that don't happen every day.
The hug you get when they realise there's something wrong,
The support you get when you need a lift,
The backing you get when life comes up against you.
All these things only come from one group that's really important in your life,
That group of people that hardly ever let you down.
They're there for you when you need them
And even when things are going right,
They're there for you when you don't ask them to be.
One of the most important things in life is to have your second family,
The family, not made up of your blood relatives,
But made up of your friends.

So, this group of people shouldn't be taken for granted,
They're your friends because they've chosen to be,
Not because they have to.
Keep them close to your heart,
No matter what happens with other relationships and family problems
They'll always be there for you.
So the next time you hear the 'hi' in the corridor,
Or get that hug when you're feeling down,
Remember, friends are one of the most important things in your life,
Don't take them for granted!

Rebekah Morris (16)

A Snail Is . . .

A slow old man,
A slimy puddle of goo
And a slithery old snake.

Slow traffic in a jam,
A slippery block of ice
And a slippery old worm.

A slow Mr Bean - old banger,
A slippery bar of soap
And a slithery lizard.

A big hard rock,
A little bouncy ball,
A swirly ice cream.

A slug with a shell,
A shell with a slug
And a monster in the cabbage patch.

A silver thread,
An artist's design,
A sparkle of a star.

A slow snail,
A slimy snail,
A slithery snail.

A hard snail shell,
A swirly snail,
Pretty much it's a snail!

Andrew Richard Wilson (11)

Kilkeel High School

The Moon Is . . .

A big ball of cheese,
A ball with holes in it,
A big yellow ball,
A big yellow light bulb,
Grandpa Simpson's head,
A beach ball that never comes down,
A yellow jawbreaker for a giant,
A big pot of gold,
A big scoop of vanilla ice cream,
My yellow hoodie,
A king's crown,
A yellow pepper,
A gold ring,
A pound coin,
A big yellow bouncy ball,
Nani's football boots,
Mrs Matthew's flowerpot,
A big sunflower,
A fireman's hat,
An egg yolk,
A banana,
A lemon,
A haystack,
A yellow football.

Andre Waddell (12)

The Sun Is . . .

The sun is . . .
A yellow sunflower,
A golden ball in the sky,
A lovely goldfish,
A beautiful yellow rose,
Yellow fairy dust glittering in the sky,
A gorgeous ring,
A yellow balloon,
A yellow bee,
The sun is . . .
A yellow firework,
A yellow hairband,
Toffee popcorn,
A yellow T-shirt,
A bright star,
A hot fire,
Yellow chewing gum,
A beautiful dress,
A light bulb,
A blinding light,
A yellow highlighter,
A warm island,
A glory for all
And a delight for me.

Naomi McConnell (11)

Untitled

Not the tidiest of people
Rough and dirty
Doesn't seem to care
Knows his own mind
Takes nothing into consideration
Long, greasy hair
Like an old man
That's just his style
Hot-headed
Can be set off by the slightest thing
Can seem to smile
Doesn't look very smart
But has common sense
No fashion
Disgracefully messy.

David Aplin (14)

My Bright Blue Tractor

I open the shed door,
It's there,
Shining into my dark red pupils,
I stamp my feet on the steps as I climb in,
I land on the seat,
The door slams shut!
My blue jumper,
I am camouflaged,
The engine nags at me,
She wants me to let my anger out,
My bright blue tractor.

Jonathan Annett (14)

My Pen

Red
From Cyprus
You can hear him clicking
Looks quite fancy
But not too fancy
I see him almost every day
Except for Sundays
I never see him then
He probably knows my hand better than me
But now he has passed away.

Alan Graham (13)

A Brilliant Midfielder

A brilliant midfielder
Scoring lots of goals
He's a brilliant passer
And can play wicked balls.

He links up well with Walcott
And hits some wicked shots,
He does everything so easily
Playing like he was a robot.

He can shoot with power
He can score with both feet
He plays for the best team in the world
And helps his goalkeeper keep a clean sheet.

Cesc Fabregas - Arsenal.

Matthew Burns (12)

King Cobra

The slithery snake slithers silently through the tall green grass.
His large head shooting on in the direction of his head.
His excitement clearly rising
As he tastes the air with his forked tongue
So he can locate his next victim.
The cheetah of the reptile world
This is because of his speed.
The vibration of his menacing hiss
Sends waves through his territory.
His poisonous fangs paralyse his defenceless victims,
Then with his unhinged jaws
He swallows them whole,
In one minute flat.

Chloe Hanna (12)

Summer

In the summer the sun didn't come,
The weather was so wet.
We learned to water skate,
Took the wheels off our skateboards
And down the road we slid on our boards.
Like bats out of hell,
We swished along, soaked from our heads to our toes.
Mum would shout,
'What are you doing?'
As the rain fell like liquid sunshine
We skated on past like we had no care in the world
And the rain was warm.
But then!
The sun came up and dried up all our water,
'No! No!' we would shout!
Mum was very cheerful that day,
That was how summer was spent!

Laura Annett (12)

Twin Towers

One day people found a reason to cry.
Their loved ones' lives were cut too short.
A terrorist plane crashed through the glass
Like a rocket flying into space.
The smoke kept rising up and up
As people were trapped, trying to keep calm,
But inside crying for help.
Sirens blaring, people screaming.
Not knowing what to do or think,
Wanting to escape the two buildings that were collapsing,
Hitting the ground . . . with a big *bang!*
Thousands of families sat in their homes,
Mourning the deaths of those who just happened to be
In the wrong place, at the wrong time.
The night sky covered the city like a blanket
As the moon shone on those sad homes
As if God sent an angel
To watch over them
And keep them safe.

Michelle Hamilton (12)

9/11

All was quiet in New York,
Everyone was fine,
But then there came a dreadful moment,
That played with everyone's mind.
Two planes flew overhead,
Sadly both had been hijacked,
The airline knew but sadly
There was nothing they could do
When *boom!*
They all looked up to see
As the bang echoed through the town
One of the plane's flew into a tower
That had a twin right beside it,
They were all screaming and crying too, to keep everyone safe,
A ball of flames out from it,
They all knew that now they were dead
But then everyone noticed
That the second plane had crashed too,
They were devastated and worrying too,
You see they knew that one plane was gone but the other wasn't
But then that all changed
Another ball of flames switched on again.
They knew it was their time to die,
But they all knew who was to blame.
This is a story that made New York known
But it was a tragic day named the 9/11.

Dean Hammond (13)

The Drum

I am a drum,
I have two snares,
I am really loud,
You will hear the thud of your heart,
You can do triplets on me,
You can hear me from a mile away,
I have a brilliant bounce,
My skins are really tight,
I have a brilliant pair of sticks with me.

Jordan Mullan (13)

Time Goes By!

What am I?
I am easily wound up.
I never stop ticking.
I do as I please.
All eyes are on me.
You see me everywhere.
Try to keep track of me.
I'm never on your side.
I am a grandfather clock!

Louise Warnock (12)

A Biography Of A Television!

You can change my moods
By pressing my buttons.
Very loud.
Very expensive
But fragile.
Loud in the daytime
But quiet in the night
Like bright colours.
Do different things
At different times.
Small and shiny.

Lucy Aplin (12)

A Very Bouncy Ball

I sparkle and shine,
Very decorative and smothered in bright colours.
I grow ecstatic at the smallest things,
So I get worn out while I bounce about.
I can get so mad!
I hit the ceiling!
When you use me too much
I get tired.
I am a very bouncy ball!

Alexandra Moore (12)

My Sparkly, Fashionable Top

I am a bright, stunning glittery top!
I like to be fashionable, it has a fashionable sparkle.
I am also multicoloured because I have all different moods and thoughts.
I wear different tops each day depending what I feel like
And what mood I am in each day.
You can get nice tops and ugly tops but it's sometimes how I feel!
My top always stands out from the crowd
Because it's unique like me in my own special way.
My top is decorated and soft on the inside and on the outside.
I love fashion!

Anna Graham (12)

Surprise, Surprise

I'm ready to bust,
I am filled to the brim.
I am full,
My zip-worn and rusty,
I'm multicoloured and have vertical strips,
Inside is a sharpener to sharpen my ideas,
It is a friend that is always there,
I am like a bullet of information,
It is a working machine like me,
When opened there is a surprise,
I am a pencil case.

Christopher Wilson (13)

Fish

Trees, trees in this place,
My home this is,
Perils I do face,
So I keep on swimming!

I swim all day,
In a glass tank,
I was put there back in May,
So I keep on swimming!

They gave me a name,
I'm called Finn,
They hope to make me tame,
So I keep on swimming.

I've made some mates,
Some of them not so nice,
I don't want to be the bait,
So I keep on swimming!

The giant comes tap, tap, tap,
I'm not hungry 'cause,
I am hiding having a nap,
So I keep on swimming!

Here she comes to clean the house,
Clean, clean, clean,
I hope she doesn't find the mouse,
So I keep on swimming!

Some friends come and then they go,
In comes the undertaker like a thief,
Then I feel so very low,
But I keep on swimming!

Lynn Campbell (13)

A Very Loud CD Player

Loud so everyone can hear me.
I play music.
Moving and dancing.
Good standards
And quality.
I like to be noticed
In ways as a good person.
People can rely
On me.
People listen to me.
I am small,
So it's hard for people to hear me.

Amy Burden (12)

A Big Bed

I'm a big double bed,
A comfy mattress,
That will not break,
A cosy duvet,
Keeps you warm,
Lots of pillows,
Keep you comfy,
A big strong wooden frame,
I can take a heavy load,
I'm here for you,
I'll take you to a dream world,
Lift you up into the atmosphere,
Whirl around the world,
Faster, faster,
Then suddenly,
Start falling,
Faster, faster,
Until you thud,
Then wake up
Sweating on your bedroom floor!

David John Goodwin (12)

This Is One Of My Favourite Things

I am sometimes lazy and slow.
I am as light as a feather.
I can be like a friend because I am carried about a lot.
If I'm angry my screen will pop!
If I am switched on too long I can overheat.
I am as clean as a whistle.
I can do anything from A-Z.
The screen will dim if the battery is low.
I'm not like a computer because you do not need a lead running to the hard drive.
I am a laptop, brainy and fast to load!

Glenn Wright (13)

My Red 414

I open the shed door,
It is reflecting in the dark,
I walk over to it,
Sit on the seat,
Can't wait to pull the lever,
It awakes and bounces away.
Down a hill, over a bridge,
I wreck about on it on a field,
Come home quickly with a dirty tractor,
Drive the tractor into the shed,
Shut the door and then . . .

Richard Annett (13)

My Best Friend!

A Hallowe'en pumpkin,
Smile used often,
Shows me new dances,
Things she wouldn't tell anyone else,
A passion for animals,
Hang out at my house or hers,
Hear her silvery laugh a mile away,
Stripy tops, sparkly tops, checked tops,
Lots of tops!
What can I say about her shoes . . .
Whoo, I love them!

Lynne Graham (13)

Kilkeel High School

My Dog Tess . . .

My dog Tess . . . the best dog ever.
Very hyper.
Can't sit still.
She spies me and gallops at me.
Gives me a hug.
Loves to get fussed over.
Very protective of my wee sister.
Jet-black hair.
Golden on legs and chest.
I adore her giant paws -
Cream and look like socks.
Got her on Christmas Day.
Best present *ever!*

Laura McConnell (13)

The Jump

My head emptied and filled with air,
The dark scarlet helmet on my head shone radiantly in the sun.
As my parachute tightly clung to me like a koala,
Butterflies danced in the depth of my stomach,
Shivers captured every nerve on my body.

A thousand miles up didn't seem much to a kite,
But my whole body tingled with a surprising sensation.
As I prepared to take the leap of my life,
My knees knocked in frantic delight, my body screamed in fright
And sweat clothed me in a blanket of fear.

One, two, three . . . *jump!*
My whole body was flying free,
I was a puppet without the strings.
My heart bounced around me like a child's bouncy ball,
As all my blood was pushed to my head and I began to fall, back into the world.

Janice Graham (16)

Dust Arthur - Kilkeel High School

Pressure

Suffocating expectations,
Words of wisdom choke me.
A rush of energy that gives me a shiver,
Silenced by internal thought.

Like a time bomb, ready to blow,
A rush I can control.
A cold sweat on my forehead
And a warmth I can't control.

The walls are closing in,
Nobody to blame but myself.
The walls turn to rubble
And I crack under the pressure.

David Henning (17)

He Who Laughs

A sadistic genius' fantasy
Too young to be appreciated
Mockery anticipated.

A desire for death
Madness the next step
An appalling achievement
To laugh in the face of the Reaper.

Who invented this lethal criminal?
Immortal, yet wanting to die.
Feeding only from Man's weakest moments.

Tongue scraping across a scarlet blade.
Grotesque yellow teeth radiate
Into giggling hysterics
As another victim stumbles to the ground.

I laugh when I am free
I laugh when I am caged
I'll laugh when the world burns.
I am madness
I am not afraid.

Claudia Green (16)

Kilkeel High School

The Match!

I wake up as excited as ever about the match,
I get ready for the match and put my ever faithful football shirt on,
Then straight to the local café for a big greasy fry-up with my mates,
With the taste of fried egg still in my mouth we make our way to the stadium,
With a short stop in the local pub for a pint or two,
Then it's off to the match we go,
We go through the old squeaky turnstiles,
As soon as we walk out the back of the stand we can smell the burgers sizzling,
We can hear people shouting, 'Programmes for sale, only £2!'
I go to the old damp, smelly toilets,
Then we find our old wooden painted seats,
The teams walk out and you can feel the buzz around the stadium,
The atmosphere becomes electric as the match kicks off,
The crowd are in singing voice with the chants getting louder and louder,
This is the biggest ever match our wee country has ever seen.

Aaron Parke (15)

The Dark

Seeing is believing but not in the dark
When you can't trust your eyes to prove your ears or heart.
You force yourself to cover your head
And try to believe that nothing is there.
You can't wait for dawn to bring light,
When darkness flees and you can trust your sight.
Fear and darkness go hand in hand
But only one has conquered Man.

Ashley Cracknell (18)

Nothing

Will they laugh when I'm in an early grave?
Will they keep jeering at me when I'm dead?
Some give me a smile to show that they care
But their smiles are no more than empty love.
Alone with only a blade for comfort,
I want to feel pain to know that I'm alive
So I know that this nightmare is my life.

My numb heart speeds its duty as blade and skin touch.
My vision blurs as pointless tears fill my eyes.
I apply pressure, I cringe, I bleed.
I raise my arm and watch life drizzle down.
The streams of red turn to drips at my elbow.
They destroy the purity of the white tiles
Like my life, as laughter turns my heart black.

I need to slice again to get another fix.
I apply more pressure, I cringe, I bleed.
This is my euphoria. I feel weightless.
My sight blurs again; I wipe away the tears.
The room spins around me.
The drips are now a lake.

I collapse; I inhale to scream
But running from lions never seemed so pointless.
If I survive, what is there to live for?
I don't want to die, but I don't want to live.
I'm left in blackness.
I feel weak. I feel helpless. I feel despair.
I feel nothing.

John Finlay (17)

Summer Weather . . .

The cold, relentless rain
Was forced and beaten,
By the fierce angry wind.
The ageing, on-looking mountains,
With the dull lamenting clouds engulfing them,
Stared down depressingly on all around.
Rivers foamed and roared,
With the ferocity of the ravaging waters.
The much desired face of the sun
Was rarely and briefly spotted.

No, family trips to the seaside,
No romantic summer evening walks.
Naught but cold and rain.

But; the dreaded ringing of the school bell,
Called on high to the sun
And behold, it came, in all its glorious beauty.
As the skies were happily brightened.
So too, were our faces.
Our light filled eyes glared,
Upon all they had been desperate for . . .
The summer weather!

James McConnell (16)

Young Writers Information

We hope you have enjoyed reading this book - and that you will continue to enjoy it in the coming years.

If you like reading and writing poetry drop us a line, or give us a call, and we'll send you a free information pack.

Alternatively if you would like to order further copies of this book or any of our other titles, then please give us a call or log onto our website at www.youngwriters.co.uk

Young Writers Information
Remus House
Coltsfoot Drive
Peterborough
PE2 9JX
(01733) 890066